SCANNERS LIVE IN VAIN

CORDWAINER SMITH

SCANNERS LIVE IN VAIN

Nadakkavu, Kozhikode, Kerala, 673011
www.insightpublica.com
e-mail: insightpublica@gmail.com

Title: **SCANNERS LIVE IN VAIN**
Author: **CORDWAINER SMITH**
First Insight Edition: August 2024
Copyright © Reserved
All rights reserved.
Printed and Published by
InsightinPublica Printers & Publishers Pvt. Ltd.
ISBN: 978-93-5517-768-1

contents

SCANNERS LIVE IN VAIN

CORDWAINER SMITH

This story deals with science-fiction's oldest subject—space-travel. Yet the author's treatment of the subject is so completely different that it makes "SCANNERS" one of the most outstanding stories to appear in any magazine!

Martel was angry. He did not even adjust his blood away from anger. He stamped across the room by judgment, not by sight. When he saw the table hit the floor, and could tell by the expression on Luci's face that the table must have made a loud crash, he looked down to see if his leg were broken. It was not. Scanner to the core, he had to scan himself. The action was reflex and automatic. The inventory included his legs, abdomen, Chestbox of instruments, hands, arms, face and back with the Mirror. Only then did Martel go back to being angry. He talked with his voice, even though he knew that his wife hated its blare and preferred to have him write.

"I tell you, I must cranch. I have to cranch. It's my worry, isn't it?"

When Luci answered, he saw only a part of her words as he read her lips: "Darling ... you're my husband ... right to love you ... dangerous ... do it ... dangerous ... wait ...."

He faced her, but put sound in his voice, letting the blare hurt her again: "I tell you, I'm going to cranch."

Catching her expression, he became rueful and a little tender: "Can't you understand what it means to me? To get out of this horrible prison in my own head? To be feel again—to feel my feet on the ground, to feel the air a man again—hearing your voice, smelling smoke? To move against my face? Don't you know what it means?"

Her wide-eyed worrisome concern thrust him back into pure annoyance. He read only a few words as her lips moved: "... love you ... your own good ... don't you think I want you to be human? ... your own good ... too much ... he said ... they said ...."

When he roared at her, he realized that his voice must be particularly bad. He knew that the sound hurt her no less than did the words: "Do you think I wanted you to marry a Scanner? Didn't I tell you we're almost as low as the habermans? We're dead, I tell you. We've got to be dead to do our work. How can anybody go to the Up-and-Out? Can you dream what raw Space is? I warned you. But you married me. All right, you married a man. Please, darling, let me be a man. Let me hear your voice, let me feel the warmth of being alive, of being human. Let me!"

He saw by her look of stricken assent that he had won the argument. He did not use his voice again. Instead, he pulled his tablet up from where it hung against his chest. He wrote on it, using the pointed fingernail of his right forefinger—the Talking Nail of a Scanner—in quick cleancut script: "Pls, drlng, whrs Crnching Wire?"

She pulled the long gold-sheathed wire out of the pocket of her apron. She let its field sphere fall to the carpeted floor. Swiftly, dutifully, with the deft obedience of a Scanner's wife, she wound the Cranching Wire around his head, spirally around his neck and chest. She avoided the instruments set in his chest. She even avoided the radiating scars around the instruments, the stigmata of men who had gone Up and into the Out. Mechanically he lifted a foot as she slipped the wire between his feet. She drew the wire taut. She snapped the small plug into the High Burden Control next to his Heart Reader. She helped him to sit down, arranging his hands for him, pushing his head back into the cup at the top of the chair. She turned then, full-face toward him, so that he could read her lips easily. Her expression was composed.

She knelt, scooped up the sphere at the other end of the wire, stood erect calmly, her back to him. He scanned her, and saw nothing in her posture but grief which would have escaped the eye of anyone but a Scanner. She spoke: he could see her chest-muscles moving. She realized that she was not facing him, and turned so that he could see her lips.

"Ready at last?"

He smiled a yes.

She turned her back to him again. (Luci could never bear to watch him Under-the-wire.) She tossed the wiresphere into the air. It caught in the force-field, and hung there. Suddenly it glowed. That was all. All—except for the sudden red stinking roar of coming back to his senses. Coming back, across the wild threshold of pain.

I

When he awakened under the wire, he did not feel as though he had just cranched. Even though it was the second cranching within the week, he felt fit. He lay in the chair. His ears drank in the sound of air touching things in the room. He heard Luci breathing in the next room, where she was hanging up the wire to cool. He smelt the thousand-and-one smells that are in anybody's room: the crisp freshness of the germ-burner, the sour-sweet tang of the humidifier, the odor of the dinner they had just eaten, the smells of clothes, furniture, of people themselves. All these were pure delight. He sang a phrase or two of his favorite song:

"Here's to the haberman, Up and Out!

"Up—oh!—and Out—oh!—Up and Out!..."

He heard Luci chuckle in the next room. He gloated over the sounds of her dress as she swished to the doorway.

She gave him her crooked little smile. "You sound all right. Are you all right, really?"

Even with this luxury of senses, he scanned. He took the flash-quick inventory which constituted his professional skill. His eyes swept in the news of the instruments. Nothing showed off scale, beyond the Nerve Compression hanging in the edge of "Danger." But he could not worry about the Nerve box. That always came through Cranching. You couldn't get under the wire without having it show on the Nerve box. Some day the box would go to Overload and drop back down to Dead. That was the way a haberman ended. But you couldn't have everything. People who went to the Up-and-Out had to pay the price for Space.

Anyhow, he should worry! He was a Scanner. A good one, and he knew it. If he couldn't scan himself, who could? This cranching wasn't too dangerous. Dangerous, but not too dangerous.

Luci put out her hand and ruffled his hair as if she had been reading his thoughts, instead of just following them: "But you know you shouldn't have! You shouldn't!"

"But I did!" He grinned at her.

Her gaiety still forced, she said: "Come on, darling, let's have a good time. I have almost everything there is in the icebox—all your favorite tastes. And I have two new records just full of smells. I tried them out myself, and even I liked them. And you know me—"

"Which?"

"Which what, you old darling?"

He slipped his hand over her shoulders as he limped out of the room. (He could never go back to feeling the floor beneath his feet, feeling the air against his face, without being bewildered and clumsy. As if cranching was real, and being a haberman was a bad dream. But he was a haberman, and a Scanner.) "You know what I meant, Luci.... the smells, which you have. Which one did you like, on the record?"

"Well-l-l," said she, judiciously, "there were some lamb chops that were the strangest things—"

He interrupted: "What are lambtchots?"

"Wait till you smell them. Then guess. I'll tell you this much. It's a smell hundreds and hundreds of years old. They found about it in the old books."

"Is a lambtchot a Beast?"

"I won't tell you. You've got to wait," she laughed, as she helped him sit down and spread his tasting dishes before him. He wanted to go back over the dinner first, sampling all the pretty things he had eaten, and savoring them this time with his now-living lips and tongue.

When Luci had found the Music Wire and had thrown its sphere up into the force-field, he reminded her of the new smells. She took out the long glass records and set the first one into a transmitter.

"Now sniff!"

A queer frightening, exciting smell came over the room. It seemed like nothing-in this world, nor like anything from the Up-and-Out. Yet it was familiar. His mouth watered. His pulse beat a little faster; he scanned his Heart box. (Faster, sure enough.) But that smell, what was it? In mock perplexity, he grabbed her hands, looked into her eyes, and growled:

"Tell me, darling! Tell me, Or I'll eat you up!"

"That's just right!"

"What?"

"You're right. It should make you want to eat me. It's meat."

"Meat. Who?"

"Not a person," said she, knowledgeably, "a beast. A beast which people used to eat. A lamb was a small sheep—you've seen sheep out in the Wild, haven't you?—and a chop is part of its middle—here!" She pointed at her chest.

Martel did not hear her. All his boxes had swung over toward Alarm, some to Danger. He fought against the roar of his own mind, forcing his body into excess excitement. How easy it was to be a Scanner when you really stood outside your own body, haberman-fashion, and looked back into it with your eyes alone. Then you could manage the body, rule it coldy even in the enduring agony of Space. But to realize that you were a body, that this thing was ruling you, that the mind could kick the flesh and send it roaring off into panic! That was bad.

He tried to remember the days before he had gone into the Haberman Device, before he had been cut apart for the Up-and-Out. Had he always been subject to the rush of his emotions from his mind to his body, from his body back to his mind, confounding him so that he couldn't Scan? But he hadn't been a Scanner then.

He knew what had hit him. Amid the roar of his own pulse, he knew. In the nightmare of the Up-and-Out, that smell had forced its way through to him, while their ship burned off Venus and the habermans fought the collapsing metal with their bare hands. He had scanned then: all were in Danger. Chestboxes went up to Overload and dropped to Dead all around him as he had moved from man to man, shoving the drifting corpses out of his way as he fought to scan each man in turn, to clamp vises on unnoticed broken legs, to snap the Sleeping Valve on men whose instruments showed they were hopelessly near overload. With men trying to work and

     SCANNERS LIVE IN VAIN

cursing him for a Scanner while he, professional zeal aroused, fought to do his job and keep them alive in the Great Pain of Space, he had smelled that smell. It had fought its way along his rebuilt nerves, past the Haberman cuts, past all the safeguards of physical and mental discipline. In the wildest hour of tragedy, he had smelled aloud. He remembered it was like a bad cranching, connected with the fury and nightmare all around him. He had even stopped his work to scan himself, fearful that the First Effect might come, breaking past all Haberman cuts and ruining him with the Pain of Space. But he had come through. His own instruments stayed and stayed at Danger, without nearing Overload. He had done his job, and won a commendation for it. He had even forgotten the burning ship.

All except the smell.

And here the smell was all over again—the smell of meat-with-fire....

Luci looked at him with wifely concern. She obviously thought he had cranched too much, and was about to haberman back. She tried to be cheerful: "You'd better rest, honey."

He whispered to her: "Cut—off—that—smell."

She did not question his word. She cut the transmitter. She even crossed the room and stepped up the room controls until a small breeze flitted across the floor and drove the smells up to the ceiling.

He rose, tired and stiff. (His instruments were normal, except that Heart was fast and Nerves still hanging on the edge of Danger.) He spoke sadly:

"Forgive me, Luci. I suppose I shouldn't have cranched. Not so soon again. But darling, I have to get out from being a haberman. How can I ever be near you? How can I be a man—not hearing my own voice, not even feeling my own life as it goes through my veins? I love you, darling. Can't I ever be near you?"

Her pride was disciplined and automatic: "But you're a Scanner!"

"I know I'm a Scanner. But so what?"

She went over the words, like a tale told a thousand times to reassure herself: "You are the bravest of the brave, the most skilful of the skilled. All Mankind owes most honor to the Scanner, who unites the Earths of Mankind. Scanners are the protectors of the Habermans. They are the judges in the Up-and Out. They make men live in the place where men need desperately to die. They are the most honored of Mankind, and even the Chiefs of the Instrumentality are delighted to pay them homage!"

With obstinate sorrow he demurred: "Luci, we've heard that all before. But does it pay us back—"

"'Scanners work for more than pay. They are the strong guards of Mankind.' Don't you remember that?"

"But our lives, Luci. What can you get out of being the wife of a Scanner? Why did you marry me? I'm human only when I cranch. The rest of the time—you know what I am. A machine. A man turned into a machine. A man who has been killed and kept alive for duty. Don't you realize what I miss?"

"Of course, darling, of course—"

He went on: "Don't you think I remember my childhood? Don't you think I remember what it is to be a man and not a haberman? To walk and feel my feet on the ground? To feel a decent clean pain instead of watching my body every minute to see if I'm alive? How will I know if I'm dead? Did you ever think of that, Luci? How will I know if I'm dead?"

She ignored the unreasonableness of his outburst. Pacifyingly, she said: "Sit down, darling. Let me make you some kind of a drink. You're over-wrought."

Automatically, he scanned: "No I'm not! Listen to me. How do you think it feels to be in the Up-and-Out with the crew tied-for-space all around you? How do you think it feels to watch them sleep? How do you think I like scanning, scanning, scanning month after month, when I can feel the pain-of-Space beating against every part of my body, trying to get past my Haberman blocks? How do you think I like to wake the men when I have to, and have them hate me for it? Have you ever seen habermans fight—strong men fighting, and neither knowing pain, fighting until one touches Overload? Do you think about that, Luci?" Triumphantly he added: "Can you blame me if I cranch, and come back to being a man, just two days a month?"

"I'm not blaming you, darling. Let's enjoy your cranch. Sit down now, and have a drink."

He was sitting down, resting his face in his hands, while she fixed the drink, using natural fruits out of bottles in addition to the secure alkaloids. He watched her restlessly and pitied her for marrying a scanner; and then, though it was unjust, resented having to pity her.

Just as she turned to hand him the drink, they both jumped a little as the phone rang. It should not have rung. They had turned it off. It rang again, obviously on the emergency circuit. Stepping ahead of Luci, Martel strode over to the phone and looked into it. Vomact was looking at him.

The custom of Scanners entitled him to be brusque, even with a Senior Scanner, on certain given occasions. This was one.

Before Vomact could speak, Martel spoke two words into the plate, not caring whether the old man could read lips or not:

"Cranching. Busy."

He cut the switch and went back to Luci.

The phone rang again.

Luci said, gently, "I can find out what it is, darling. Here, take your drink and sit down."

"Leave it alone," said her husband. "No one has a right to call when I'm cranching. He knows that. He ought to know that."

The phone rang again. In a fury, Martel rose and went to the plate. He cut it back on. Vomact was on the screen. Before Martel could speak, Vomact held up his Talking Nail in line with his Heartbox. Martel reverted to discipline:

"Scanner Martel present and waiting, sir."

The lips moved solemnly: "Top emergency."

"Sir, I am under the wire."

"Top emergency."

"Sir, don't you understand?" Martel mouthed his words, so he could be sure that Vomact followed. "I .... am .... under .... the .... wire. Unfit, for ... Space!"

Vomact repeated: "Top emergency. Report to your central tie-in."

"But, sir, no emergency like this—"

"Right, Martel. No emergency like this, ever before. Report to tie-in." With a faint glint of kindliness, Vomact added: "No need to de-cranch. Report as you are."

This time it was Martel whose phone was cut out. The screen went gray.

He turned to Luci. The temper had gone out of his voice. She came to him. She kissed him, and rumpled his hair. All she could say was,

"I'm sorry."

She kissed him again, knowing his disappointment. "Take good care of yourself, darling. I'll wait."

He scanned, and slipped into his transparent aircoat. At the window he paused, and waved. She called, "Good luck!" As the air flowed past him he said to himself, "This is the first time I've felt flight in—eleven years. Lord, but it's easy to fly if you can feel yourself live!"

Central Tie-in glowed white and austere far ahead. Martel peered. He saw no glare of incoming ships from the Up-and-Out, no shuddering flare of Space-fire out of control. Everything was quiet, as it should be on an off-duty night.

And yet Vomact had called. He had called an emergency higher than Space. There was no such thing. But Vomact had called it.

2

When Martel got there, he found about half the Scanners present, two dozen or so of them. He lifted the Talking finger. Most of the Scanners were standing face to face, talking in pairs as they read lips. A few of the old, impatient ones were scribbling on their Tablets and then thrusting the Tablets into other people's faces. All the faces wore the dull dead relaxed look of a haberman. When Martel entered the room, he knew that most of the others laughed in the deep isolated privacy of their own minds, each thinking things it would be useless to express in formal words. It had been a long time since a Scanner showed up at a meeting cranched.

Vomact was not there: probably, thought Martel, he was still on the phone calling others. The light of the phone flashed on and off; the bell rang. Martel felt odd when he realized that of all those present, he was the only one to hear that loud bell. It made him realize why ordinary people did not like to be around groups of habermans or Scanners. Martel looked around for company.

His friend Chang was there, busy explaining to some old and testy Scanner that he did not know why Vomact had called. Martel looked further and saw Parizianski. He walked over, threading his way past the others with a dexterity that showed he could feel his feet from the inside, and did not have to watch them. Several of the others stared at him with their dead faces, and tried to smile. But they lacked full muscular control and their faces twisted into horrid masks. (Scanners knew better than to show expression on faces which they could no longer govern. Martel added to himself, I swear I'll never smile again unless I'm cranched.)

Parizianski gave him the sign of the Talking Finger. Looking face to face, he spoke:

"You come here cranched?"

Parizianski could not hear his own voice, so the words roared like the words on a broken and screeching phone; Martel was startled, but knew that the inquiry was well meant. No one could be better-natured than the burly Pole.

"Vomact called. Top emergency."

"You told him you were cranched?"

"Yes."

"He still made you come?"

"Yes."

"Then all this—it is not for Space? You could not go Up-and-Out? You are like ordinary men?"

"That's right."

"Then why did he call us?" Some pre-Haberman habit made Parizianski wave his arms in inquiry. The hand struck the back of the old man behind them. The slap could be heard throughout the room, but only Martel heard it. Instinctively, he scanned Parizianski and the old Scanner: they scanned him back, and then asked why. Only then did the old man ask why Martel had scanned him. When Martel explained that he was under-the-wire, the old man moved swiftly away to pass on the news that there was a cranched Scanner present at the Tie-in.

Even this minor sensation could not keep the attention of most of the Scanners from the worry about the Top Emergency.

     SCANNERS LIVE IN VAIN

One young man, who had Scanned his first transit just the year before, dramatically interposed himself between Parizianski and Martel. He dramatically flashed his Tablet at them:

Is Vmct mad?

The older men shook their heads. Martel, remembering that it had not been too long that the young man had been haberman, mitigated the dead solemnity of the denial with a friendly smile. He spoke in a normal voice, saying:

"Vomact is the Senior of Scanners. I am sure that he could not go mad. Would he not see it on his boxes first?"

Martel had to repeat the question, speaking slowly and mouthing his words before the young Scanner could understand the comment. The young man tried to make his face smile, and twisted it into a comic mask. But he took up his tablet and scribbled:

Yr rght.

Chang broke away from his friend and came over, his half-Chinese face gleaming in the warm evening. (It's strange, thought Martel that more Chinese don't become scanners. Or not so strange perhaps, if you think that they never fill their quota of habermans. Chinese love good living too much. The ones who do scan are all good ones.) Chang saw that Martel was cranched, and spoke with voice:

"You break precedents. Luci must be angry to lose you?"

"She took it well. Chang, that's strange."

"What?"

"I'm cranched, and I can hear. Your voice sounds all right. How did you learn to talk like—like an ordinary person?"

"I practised with soundtracks. Funny you noticed it. I think I am the only Scanner in or between the Earths who can pass for an Ordinary Man. Mirrors and sound-tracks. I found out how to act."

"But you don't....?"

"No. I don't feel, or taste, or hear, or smell things, any more than you do. Talking doesn't do me much good. But I notice that it cheers up the people around me."

"It would make a difference in the life of Luci."

Chang nodded sagely. "My father insisted on it. He said, 'You may be proud of being a Scanner. I am sorry you are not a Man. Conceal your defects.' So I tried. I wanted to tell the old boy about the Up and Out, and what we did there, but it did not matter. He said, 'Airplanes were good enough for Confucius, and they are for me too.' The old humbug! He tries so hard to be a Chinese when he can't even read Old Chinese. But he's got wonderful good sense, and for somebody going on two hundred he certainly gets around."

Martel smiled at the thought: "In his airplane?"

Chang smiled back. This discipline of his facial muscles was amazing; a bystander would not think that Chang was a haberman, controlling his eyes, cheeks, and lips by cold intellectual control. The expression had the spontaneity of life. Martel felt a flash of envy for Chang when he looked at the dead cold faces of Parizianski and the others. He knew that he himself looked fine: but why shouldn't he? he was cranched. Turning to Parizianski he said,

"Did you see what Chang said about his father? The old boy uses an airplane."

Parizianski made motions with his mouth, but the sounds meant nothing. He took up his tablet and showed it to Martel and Chang.

Bzz bzz. Ha ha. Gd ol' boy.

At that moment, Martel heard steps out in the corridor. He could not help looking toward the door. Other eyes followed the direction of his glance.

Vomact came in.

The group shuffled to attention in four parallel lines.

   SCANNERS LIVE IN VAIN

They scanned one another. Numerous hands reached across to adjust the electrochemical controls on chestboxes which had begun to load up. One Scanner held out a broken finger which his counter-Scanner had discovered, and submitted it for treatment and splinting.

Vomact had taken out his Staff of Office. The cube at the top flashed red light through the room, the lines reformed, and all Scanners gave the sign meaning

Present and ready!

Vomact countered with the stance signifying, I am the Senior and take Command.

Talking fingers rose in the counter-gesture, We concur and commit ourselves.

Vomact raised his right arm, dropped the wrist as though it were broken, in a queer searching gesture, meaning: Any men around? Any habermans not tied? All clear for the Scanners?

Alone of all those present, the cranched Martel heard the queer rustle of feet as they all turned completely around without leaving position, looking sharply at one another and flashing their beltlights into the dark corners of the great room. When again they faced Vomact, he made a further sign:

All clear. Follow my words.

Martel noticed that he alone relaxed. The others could not know the meaning of relaxation with the minds blocked off up there in their skulls, connected only with the eyes, and the rest of the body connected with the mind only by controlling non-sensory nerves and the instrument boxes on their chests. Martel realized that, cranched as he was, he expected to hear Vomact's voice: the Senior had been talking for some time. No sound escaped his lips. (Vomact never bothered with sound.)

"...and when the first men to go Up and Out went to the Moon, what did they find?"

"Nothing," responded the silent chorus of lips.

"Therefore they went further, to Mars and to Venus. The ships went out year by year, but they did not come back until the Year One of Space. Then did a ship come back with the First Effect. Scanners, I ask you, what is the First Effect?"

"No one knows. No one knows."

"No one will ever know. Too many are the variables. By what do we know the First Effect?"

"By the Great Pain of Space," came the chorus.

"And by what further sign?"

"By the need, oh the need for death."

Vomact again: "And who stopped the need for death?"

"Henry Haberman conquered the first effect, in the Year 3 of Space."

"And, Scanners, I ask you, what did he do?"

"He made the habermans."

"How, O Scanners, are habermans made?"

"They are made with the cuts. The brain is cut from the heart, the lungs. The brain is cut from the ears, the nose. The brain is cut from the mouth, the belly. The brain is cut from desire, and pain. The brain is cut from the world. Save for the eyes. Save for the control of the living flesh."

"And how, O Scanners is flesh controlled?"

"By the boxes set in the flesh, the controls set in the chest, the signs made to rule the living body, the signs by which the body lives."

"How does a haberman live and live?"

"The haberman lives by control of the boxes."

"Whence come the habermans?"

Martel felt in the coming response a great roar of broken voices echoing through the room as the Scanners, habermans themselves, put sound behind their mouthings:

"Habermans are the scum of Mankind. Habermans are the weak, the cruel the credulous, and the unfit. Habermans are the sentenced-to-more-than-death. Habermans live in the mind alone. They are killed for Space but they live for Space. They master the ships that connect the earths. They live in the Great Pain while ordinary men sleep in the cold cold sleep of the transit."

"Brothers and Scanners, I ask you now: are we habermans or are we not?"

"We are habermans in the flesh. We are cut apart, brain and flesh. We are ready to go to the Up and Out. All of us have gone through the Haberman Device."

"We are habermans then?" Vomact's eyes flashed and glittered as he asked the ritual question.

Again the chorused answer was accompanied by a roar of voices heard only by Martel: "Habermans we are, and more, and more. We are the Chosen who are habermans by our own free will. We are the Agents of the Instrumentality of Mankind."

"What must the others say to us?"

"They must say to us, 'You are the bravest of the brave, the most skilful of the skilled. All mankind owes most honor to the Scanner, who unites the Earths of Mankind. Scanners are the protectors of the habermans. They are the judges in the Up-and-Out. They make men live in the place where men need desperately to die. They are the most honored of Mankind, and even the Chiefs of the Instrumentality are delighted to pay them homage!'"

Vomact stood more erect: "What is the secret duty of the Scanner?"

"To keep secret our law, and to destroy the acquirers thereof."

"How to destroy?"

"Twice to the Overload, back and Dead."

"If habermans die, what the duty then?"

The Scanners all compressed their lips for answer. (Silence was the code.) Martel, who—long familiar with the code—was a little bored with the proceedings, noticed that Chang was breathing too heavily; he reached over and adjusted Chang's Lung-control and received the thanks of Chang's eyes. Vomact observed the interruption and glared at them both. Martel relaxed, trying to imitate the dead cold stillness of the others. It was so hard to do, when you were cranched.

"If others die, what the duty then?" asked Vomact.

"Scanners together inform the Instrumentality. Scanners together accept the punishment. Scanners together settle the case."

"And if the punishment be severe?"

"Then no ships go."

"And if Scanners not be honored?"

"Then no ships go."

"And if a Scanner goes unpaid?"

"Then no ships go."

"And if the Others and the Instrumentality are not in all ways at all times mindful of their proper obligation to the Scanners?"

"Then no ships go."

"And what, O Scanners, if no ships go?"

"The Earths fall apart. The Wild comes back in. The Old Machines and the Beasts return."

"What is the known duty of a Scanner?"

"Not to sleep in the Up-and-Out."

"What is the second duty of a Scanner?"

"To keep forgotten the name of fear."

 SCANNERS LIVE IN VAIN

"What is the third duty of a Scanner?"

"To use the wire of Eustace Cranch only with care, only with moderation." Several pair of eyes looked quickly at Martel before the mouthed chorus went on. "To cranch only at home, only among friends, only for the purpose of remembering, of relaxing, or of begetting."

"What is the word of the Scanner?"

"Faithful though surrounded by death."

"What is the motto of the Scanner?"

"Awake though surrounded by silence."

"What is the work of the Scanner?"

"Labor even in the heights of the Up-and-Out, loyalty even in the depths of the Earths."

"How do you know a Scanner?"

"We know ourselves. We are dead though we live. And we Talk with the Tablet and the Nail."

"What is this Code?"

"This Code is the friendly ancient wisdom of Scanners, briefly put that we may be mindful and be cheered by our loyalty to one another."

At this point the formula should have run: "We complete the Code. Is there work or word for the Scanners?" But Vomact said, and he repeated:

"Top emergency. Top emergency."

They gave him the sign, Present and ready!

He said, with every eye straining to follow his lips:

"Some of you know the work of Adam Stone?"

Martel saw lips move, saying: "The Red Asteroid. The Other who lives at the edge of Space."

"Adam Stone has gone to the Instrumentality, claiming success for his work. He says that he has found how to Screen

Out the Pain of Space. He says that the Up-and-Out can be made safe for ordinary men to work in, to stay awake in. He says that there need be no more Scanners."

Beltlights flashed on all over the room as Scanners sought the right to speak. Vomact nodded to one of the older men. "Scanner Smith will speak."

Smith stepped slowly up into the light, watching his own feet. He turned so that they could see his face. He spoke: "I say that this is a lie. I say that Stone is a liar. I say that the Instrumentality must not be deceived."

He paused. Then, in answer to some question from the audience which most of the others did not see, he said:

"I invoke the secret duty of the Scanners."

Smith raised his right hand for Emergency Attention:

"I say that Stone must die."

3

Martel, still cranched, shuddered as he heard the boos, groans, shouts, squeaks, grunts and moans which came from the Scanners who forgot noise in their excitement and strove to make their dead bodies talk to one another's deaf ears. Beltlights flashed wildly all over the room. There was a rush for the rostrum and Scanners milled around at the top, vying for attention until Parizianski—by sheer bulk—shoved the others aside and down, and turned to mouth at the group.

"Brother Scanners, I want your eyes."

The people on the floor kept moving, with their numb bodies jostling one another. Finally Vomact stepped up in front of Parizianski, faced the others, and said:

"Scanners, be Scanners! Give him your eyes."

Parizianski was not good at public speaking. His lips moved too fast. He waved his hands, which took the eyes of the others away from his lips. Nevertheless, Martel was able to follow most of the message:

"...can't do this. Stone may have succeeded. If he has succeeded, it means the end of the Scanners. It means the end of the habermans, too. None of us will have to fight in the Up-and-Out. We won't have anybody else going under-the-Wire for a few hours or days of being human. Everybody will be Other. Nobody will have to Cranch, never again. Men can be men. The habermans can be killed decently and properly, the way men were killed in the Old Days, without anybody keeping them alive. They won't have to work in the Up-and-Out! There will be no more Great Pain—think of it! No ... more ... Great ... Pain! How do we know that Stone is a liar—" Lights began flashing directly into his eyes. (The rudest insult of Scanner to Scanner was this.)

Vomact again exercized authority. He stepped in front of Parizianski and said something which the others could not see. Parizianski stepped down from the rostrum. Vomact again spoke:

"I think that some of the Scanners disagree with our Brother Parizianski. I say that the use of the rostrum be suspended till we have had a chance for private discussion. In fifteen minutes I will call the meeting back to order."

Martel looked around for Vomact when the Senior had rejoined the group on the floor. Finding the Senior, Martel wrote swift script on his Tablet, waiting for a chance to thrust the Tablet before the Senior's eyes. He had written,

Am crcnhd. Rspctfly requst prmissn lv now, stnd by fr orders.

Being cranched did strange things to Martel Most meetings that he attended seemed formal heartening ceremonial, lighting up the dark inward eternities of habermanhood. When he was not cranched, he noticed his body no more than a marble bust notices its marble pedestal. He had stood with them before. He had stood with them effortless hours, while the long-winded ritual broke through the terrible loneliness behind his eyes, and made him feel that the Scanners, though a confraternity of the damned, were none the less forever honored by the professional requirements of their mutilation.

This time, it was different. Coming cranched, and in full possession of smell-sound-taste-feeling, he reacted more or less as a normal man would. He saw his friends and colleagues as a lot of cruelly driven ghosts, posturing out the meaningless ritual of their indefeasible damnation. What difference did anything make, once you were a haberman? Why all this talk about habermans and Scanners? Habermans were criminals or heretics, and Scanners were gentlemen-volunteers, but they were all in the same fix—except that Scanners were deemed worthy of the short-time return of the Cranching Wire, while habermans were simply disconnected while the ships lay in port and were left suspended until they should be awakened, in some hour of emergency or trouble, to work out another spell of their damnation. It was a rare haberman that you saw on the street—someone of special merit or bravery, allowed to look at mankind from the terrible prison of his own mechanified body. And yet, what Scanner ever pitied a haberman? What Scanner ever honored a haberman except perfunctorily in the line of duty? What had the Scanners as a guild and a class, ever done for the habermans, except to murder them with a twist of the wrist whenever a haberman, too long beside a Scanner, picked up the tricks of the Scanning trade and learned how to live at his own will, not the will the Scanners imposed? What could the Others, the ordinary men, know of what went on inside the ships? The Others slept in their cylinders, mercifully unconscious until they woke up on whatever other Earth they had consigned themselves to. What could the Others know of the men who had to stay alive within the ship?

What could any Other know of the Up-and-Out? What Other could look at the biting acid beauty of the stars in open

    SCANNERS LIVE IN VAIN

space? What could they tell of the Great Pain, which started quietly in the marrow, like an ache, and proceeded by the fatigue and nausea of each separate nerve cell, brain cell, touchpoint in the body, until life itself became a terrible aching hunger for silence and for death?

He was a Scanner. All right, he was a Scanner. He had been a Scanner from the moment when, wholly normal, he had stood in the sunlight before a Subchief of Instrumentality, and had sworn:

"I pledge my honor and my life to Mankind. I sacrifice myself willingly for the welfare of Mankind. In accepting the perilous austere Honor, I yield all my rights without exception to the Honorable Chiefs of the Instrumentality and to the Honored Confraternity of Scanners."

He had pledged.

He had gone into the Haberman Device.

He remembered his Hell. He had not had such a bad one, even though it had seemed to last a hundred million years, all of them without sleep. He had learned to feel with his eyes. He had learned to see despite the heavy eyeplates set back of his eyeballs, to insulate his eyes from the rest of him. He had learned to watch his skin. He still remembered the time he had noticed dampness on his shirt, and had pulled out his Scanning Mirror only to discover that he had worn a hole in his side by leaning against a vibrating machine. (A thing like that could not happen to him now; he was too adept at reading his own instruments.) He remembered the way that he had gone Up-and-Out, and the way that the Great Pain beat into him, despite the fact that his touch, smell, feeling, and hearing were gone for all ordinary purposes. He remembered killing habermans, and keeping others alive, and standing for months beside the Honorable Scanner-Pilot while neither of them slept. He remembered going ashore on Earth Four, and remembered that he had not enjoyed it, and had realized on that day that there was no reward.

Martel stood among the other Scanners. He hated their awkwardness when they moved, their immobility when they stood still. He hated the queer assortment of smells which their bodies yielded unnoticed. He hated the grunts and groans and squawks which they emitted from their deafness. He hated them, and himself.

How could Luci stand him? He had kept his chestbox reading Danger for weeks while he courted her, carrying the Cranch Wire about with him most illegally, and going direct from one cranch to the other without worrying about the fact his indicators all crept up to the edge of Overload. He had wooed her without thinking of what would happen if she did say, "Yes." She had.

"And they lived happily ever after." In Old Books they did, but how could they, in life? He had had eighteen days under-the-wire in the whole of the past year! Yet she had loved him. She still loved him. He knew it. She fretted about him through the long months that he was in the Up-and-Out. She tried to make home mean something to him even when he was haberman, make food pretty when it could not be tasted, make herself lovable when she could not be kissed—or might as well not, since a haberman body meant no more than furniture. Luci was patient.

And now, Adam Stone! (He let his Tablet fade: how could he leave, now?)

God bless Adam Stone?

Martel could not help feeling a little sorry for himself. No longer would the high keen call of duty carry him through two hundred or so years of the Other's time, two million private eternities of his own. He could slouch and relax. He could forget High Space, and let the Up-and-Out be tended by Others. He could cranch as much as he dared. He could be almost normal—almost—for one year or five years or

 SCANNERS LIVE IN VAIN

no years. But at least he could stay with Luci. He could go with her into the Wild, where there were Beasts and Old Machines still roving the dark places. Perhaps he would die in the excitement of the hunt, throwing spears at an ancient Manshonjagger as it leapt from its lair, or tossing hot spheres at the tribesmen of the Unforgiven who still roamed the Wild. There was still life to live, still a good normal death to die, not the moving of a needle out in the silence and pain of Space!

He had been walking about restlessly. His ears were attuned to the sounds of normal speech, so that he did not feel like watching the mouthings of his brethern. Now they seemed to have come to a decision. Vomact was moving to the rostrum. Martel looked about for Chang, and went to stand beside him. Chang whispered.

"You're as restless as water in mid-air! What's the matter? De-cranching?"

They both scanned Martel, but the instruments held steady and showed no sign of the cranch giving out.

The great light flared in its call to attention. Again they formed ranks. Vomact thrust his lean old face into the glare, and spoke:

"Scanners and Brothers, I call for a vote." He held himself in the stance which meant: "I am the Senior and take Command."

A beltlight flashed in protest.

It was old Henderson. He moved to the rostrum, spoke to Vomact, and—with Vomact's nod of approval—turned full-face to repeat his question:

"Who speaks for the Scanners Out in Space?"

No beltlight or hand answered.

Henderson and Vomact, face to face, conferred for a few moments. Then Henderson faced them again:

"I yield to the Senior in Command. But I do not yield to a Meeting of the Confraternity. There are sixty-eight Scanners, and only forty-seven present, of whom one is cranched and U.D. I have therefore proposed that the Senior in Command assume authority only over an Emergency Committee of the Confraternity, not over a Meeting. Is that agreed and understood by the Honorable Scanners?"

Hands rose in assent.

Chang murmured in Martel's ear, "Lot of difference that makes! Who can tell the difference between a meeting and a committee?" Martel agreed with the words, but was even more impressed with the way that Chang, while haberman, could control his own voice.

Vomact resumed chairmanship: "We now vote on the question of Adam Stone.

"First, we can assume that he has not succeeded, and that his claims are lies. We know that from our practical experience as Scanners. The Pain of Space is only part of Scanning" (But the essential part, the basis of it all, thought Martel.) "and we can rest assured that Stone cannot solve the problem of Space Discipline."

"That tripe again," whispered Chang, unheard save by Martel.

"The Space Discipline of our Confraternity has kept High Space clean of war and dispute. Sixty-eight disciplined men control all High Space. We are removed by our oath and our haberman status from all Earthly passions.

"Therefore, if Adam Stone has conquered the Pain of Space, so that Others can wreck our Confraternity and bring to Space the trouble and ruin which afflicts Earths, I say that Adam Stone is wrong. If Adam Stone succeeds, Scanners live in Vain!

"Secondly, if Adam Stone has not conquered the Pain of Space, he will cause great trouble in all the Earths. The Instrumentality and the Subchiefs may not give us as many habermans as we need to operate the ships of Mankind. There will be wild stories, and fewer recruits and, worst of all, the Discipline of the Confraternity may relax if this kind of nonsensical heresy is spread around.

"Therefore, if Adam Stone has succeeded, he threatens the ruin of the Confraternity and should die.

"I move the death of Adam Stone."

And Vomact made the sign, The Honorable Scanners are pleased to vote.

4

Martel grabbed wildly for his beltlight. Chang, guessing ahead, had his light out and ready; its bright beam, voting No, shone straight up at the ceiling. Martel got his light out and threw its beam upward in dissent. Then he looked around. Out of the forty-seven present, he could see only five or six glittering.

Two more lights went on. Vomact stood as erect as a frozen corpse. Vomact's eyes flashed as he stared back and forth over the group, looking for lights. Several more went on. Finally Vomact took the closing stance:

May it please the Scanners to count the vote.

Three of the older men went up on the rostrum with Vomact. They looked over the room. (Martel thought: These damned ghosts are voting on the life of a real man, a live man! They have no right to do it. I'll tell the Instrumentality! But he knew that he would not. He thought of Luci and what she might gain by the triumph of Adam Stone: the heartbreaking folly of the vote was then almost too much for Martel to bear.)

All three of the tellers held up their hands in unanimous agreement on the sign of the number: Fifteen against.

Vomact dismissed them with a bow of courtesy. He turned

and again took the stance, I am the Senior and take Command.

Marvelling at his own daring, Martel flashed his beltlight on. He knew that anyone of the bystanders might reach over and twist his Heartbox to Overload for such an act. He felt Chang's hand reaching to catch him by the aircoat. But he eluded Chang's grasp and ran, faster than a Scanner should, to the platform. As he ran, he wondered what appeal to make. It was no use talking commonsense. Not now. It had to be law.

He jumped up on the rostrum beside Vomact, and took the stance: Scanners, an Illegality!

He violated good custom while speaking, still in the stance: "A Committee has no right to vote death by a majority vote. It takes two-thirds of a full Meeting."

He felt Vomact's body lunge behind him, felt himself falling from the rostrum, hitting the floor, hurting his knees and his touch-aware hands. He was helped to his feet. He was scanned. Some Scanner he scarcely knew took his instruments and toned him down.

Immediately Martel felt more calm, more detached, and hated himself for feeling so.

He looked up at the rostrum. Vomact maintained the stance signifying: Order!

The Scanners adjusted their ranks. The two Scanners next to Martel took his arms. He shouted at them, but they looked away, and cut themselves off from communication altogether.

Vomact spoke again when he saw the room was quiet: "A Scanner came here cranched. Honorable Scanners, I apologize for this. It is not the fault of our great and worthy Scanner and friend, Martel. He came here under orders. I told him not to de-cranch. I hoped to spare him an unnecessary haberman. We all know how happily Martel is married, and we wish his brave experiment well. I like Martel. I respect his judgment. I wanted him here. I knew you wanted him here. But he is cranched. He is in no mood to share in the lofty business of the Scanners. I therefore propose a solution which will meet all the requirements of fairness. I propose that we rule Scanner Martel out of order for his violation of rules. This violation would be inexcusable if Martel were not cranched.

"But at the same time, in all fairness to Martel, I further propose that we deal with the points raised so improperly by our worthy but disqualified brother."

Vomact gave the sign, The Honorable Scanners are pleased to vote. Martel tried to reach his own beltlight; the dead strong hands held him tightly and he struggled in vain. One lone light shone high: Chang's, no doubt.

Vomact thrust his face into the light again: "Having the approval of our worthy Scanners and present company for the general proposal, I now move that this Committee declare itself to have the full authority of a Meeting, and that this Committee further make me responsible for all misdeeds which this Committee may enact, to be held answerable before the next full Meeting, but not before any other authority beyond the closed and secret ranks of Scanners."

Flamboyantly this time, his triumph evident, Vomact assumed the vote stance.

Only a few lights shone: far less, patently, than a minority of one-fourth.

Vomact spoke again. The light shone on his high calm forehead, on his dead relaxed cheekbones. His lean cheeks and chin were half-shadowed, save where the lower light picked up and spotlighted his mouth, cruel even in repose. (Vomact was said to be a descendant of some Ancient Lady who had traversed, in an illegitimate and inexplicable fashion, some hundreds of years of time in a single night. Her name, the Lady Vomact, had passed into legend; but her blood and her archaic lust for mastery lived on in the mute masterful body of her descendent. Martel could believe the old tales as he stared at the rostrum, wondering what untraceable mutation had left the Vomact kith as predators among mankind.) Calling loudly with the movement of his lips, but still without sound, Vomact appealed:

"The Honorable Committee is now pleased to reaffirm the sentence of death issued against the heretic and enemy, Adam Stone." Again the vote stance.

Again Chang's light shone lonely in its isolated protest.

Vomact then made his final move:

"I call for the designation of the Senior Scanner present as the manager of the sentence. I call for authorization to him to appoint executioners, one or many, who shall make evident the will and majesty of Scanners. I ask that I be accountable for the deed, and not for the means. The deed is a noble deed, for the protection of Mankind and for the honor of the Scanners; but of the means it must be said that they are to be the best at hand, and no more. Who knows the true way to kill an Other, here on a crowded and watchful earth? This is no mere matter of discharging a cylindered sleeper, no mere question of upgrading the needle of a haberman. When people die down here, it is not like the Up-and-Out. They die reluctantly. Killing within the Earth is not our usual business, O brothers and Scanners, as you know well. You must choose me to choose my agent as I see fit. Otherwise the common knowledge will become the common betrayal whereas if I alone know the responsibility, I alone could betray us, and you will not have far to look in case the Instrumentality comes searching." (What about the killer you choose? thought Martel. He too will know unless—unless you silence him forever.)

Vomact went into the stance, The Honorable Scanners are pleased to vote.

One light of protest shone; Chang's, again.

Martel imagined that he could see a cruel joyful smile on

SCANNERS LIVE IN VAIN

Vomact's dead face—the smile of a man who knew himself righteous and who found his righteousness upheld and affirmed by militant authority.

Martel tried one last time to come free.

The dead hands held. They were locked like vises until their owners' eyes unlocked them: how else could they hold the piloting month by month?

Martel then shouted: "Honorable Scanners, this is judicial murder."

No ear heard him. He was cranched, and alone.

None the less, he shouted again: "You endanger the confraternity."

Nothing happened.

The echo of his voice sounded from one end of the room to the other. No head turned. No eyes met his.

Martel realized that as they paired for talk, the eyes of the Scanners averted him. He saw that no one desired to watch his speech. He knew that behind the cold faces of his friends there lay compassion or amusement. He knew that they knew him to be cranched—absurd, normal, man-like, temporarily no Scanner. But he knew that in this matter the wisdom of Scanners was nothing. He knew that only a cranched Scanner could feel with his very blood the outrage and anger which deliberate murder would provoke among the Others. He knew that the Confraternity endangered itself, and knew that the most ancient prerogative of law was the monopoly of death. Even the Ancient Nations, in the times of the Wars, before the Beasts, before men went into the Up-and-Out—even the Ancients had known this. How did they say it? Only the State shall kill. The States were gone but the Instrumentality remained, and the Instrumentality could not pardon things which occurred within the Earths but beyond its authority. Death in Space was the business, the right of the Scanners:

how could the Instrumentality enforce its laws in a place where all men who wakened, wakened only to die in the Great Pain? Wisely did the Instrumentality leave Space to the Scanners, wisely had the Confraternity not meddled inside the Earths. And now the Confraternity itself was going to step forth as an outlaw band, as a gang of rogues as stupid and reckless as the tribes of the unforgiven!

Martel knew this because he was cranched. Had he been haberman, he would have thought only with his mind, not with his heart and guts and blood. How could the other Scanners know?

Vomact returned for the last time to the Rostrum: The Committee has met and its will shall be done. Verbally he added: "Senior among you, I ask your loyalty and your silence."

At that point, the two Scanners let his arms go. Martel rubbed his numb hands, shaking his fingers to get the circulation back into the cold fingertips. With real freedom, he began to think of what he might still do. He scanned himself: the cranching held. He might have a day. Well, he could go on even if haberman, but it would be inconvenient, having to talk with Finger and Tablet. He looked about for Chang. He saw his friend standing patient and immobile in a quiet corner. Martel moved slowly, so as not to attract any more attention to himself than could be helped. He faced Chang, moved until his face was in the light, and then articulated:

"What are we going to do? You're not going to let them kill Adam Stone, are you? Don't you realize what Stone's work will mean to us, if it succeeds? No more Scanners. No more habermans. No more Pain in the Up-and-Out. I tell you, if the others were all cranched, as I am, they would see it in a human way, not with the narrow crazy logic which they used in the meeting. We've got to stop them. How can we do it? What are we going to do? What does Parizianski think? Who

    SCANNERS LIVE IN VAIN

has been chosen?”

“Which question do you want me to answer?”

Martel laughed. (It felt good to laugh, even then; it felt like being a man.) “Will you help me?”

Chang’s eyes flashed across Martel’s face as Chang answered: “No. No. No.”

“You won’t help?”

“No.”

“Why not, Chang? Why not?”

“I am a Scanner. The vote has been taken. You would do the same if you were not in this unusual condition.”

“I’m not in an unusual condition. I’m cranched. That merely means that I see things the way that the Others would. I see the stupidity. The recklessness. The selfishness. It is murder.”

“What is murder? Have you not killed? You are not one of the Others. You are a Scanner. You will be sorry for what you are about to do, if you do not watch out.”

“But why did you vote against Vomact then? Didn’t you too see what Adam Stone means to all of us? Scanners will live in vain. Thank God for that! Can’t you see it?”

“No.”

“But you talk to me, Chang. You are my friend?”

“I talk to you. I am your friend. Why not?”

“But what are you going to do?”

“Nothing, Martel. Nothing.”

“Will you help me?”

“No,”

“Not even to save Stone?”

“No.”

“Then I will go to Parizianski for help.”

“It will do you no good.”

"Why not? He's more human than you, right now."

"He will not help you, because he has the job. Vomact designated him to kill Adam Stone."

Martel stopped speaking in mid-movement. He suddenly took the stance, I thank you, brother, and I depart.

At the window he turned and faced the room. He saw that Vomact's eyes were upon him. He gave the stance, I thank you, brother, and I depart, and added the flourish of respect which is shown when Seniors are present. Vomact caught the sign, and Martel could see the cruel lips move. He thought he saw the words "...take good care of yourself...." but did not wait to inquire. He stepped backward and dropped out the window.

Once below the window and out of sight, he adjusted his aircoat to maximum speed. He swam lazily in the air, scanning himself thoroughly, and adjusting his adrenal intake down. He then made the movement of release, and felt the cold air rush past his face like running water.

Adam Stone had to be at Chief Downport.

Adam Stone had to be there.

Wouldn't Adam Stone be surprised in the night? Surprised to meet the strangest of beings, the first renegade among Scanners. (Martel suddenly appreciated that it was of himself he was thinking. Martel the Traitor to Scanners! That sounded strange and bad. But what of Martel, the Loyal to Mankind? Was that not compensation? And if he won, he won Luci. If he lost, he lost nothing—an unconsidered and expendable haberman. It happened to be himself. But in contrast to the immense reward, to Mankind, to the Confraternity, to Luci, what did that matter?)

Martel thought to himself: "Adam Stone will have two visitors tonight. Two Scanners, who are the friends of one another." He hoped that Parizianski was still his friend.

"And the world," he added, "depends on which of us gets

there first."

Multifaceted in their brightness, the lights of Chief Downport began to shine through the mist ahead. Martel could see the outer towers of the city and glimpsed the phosphorescent Periphery which kept back the wild, whether Beasts, Machines, or the Unforgiven.

Once more Martel invoked the lords of his chance: "Help me to pass for an Other!"

5

Within the Downport, Martel had less trouble than he thought. He draped his aircoat over his shoulder so that it concealed the instruments. He took up his scanning mirror, and made up his face from the inside, by adding tone and animation to his blood and nerves until the muscles of his face glowed and the skin gave out a healthy sweat. That way he looked like an ordinary man who had just completed a long night flight.

After straightening out his clothing, and hiding his tablet within his jacket, he faced the problem of what to do about the Talking Finger. If he kept the nail, it would show him to be a Scanner. He would be respected, but he would be identified. He might be stopped by the guards whom the Instrumentality had undoubtedly set around the person of Adam Stone. If he broke the Nail— But he couldn't! No Scanner in the history of the Confraternity had ever willingly broken his nail. That would be Resignation, and there was no such thing. The only way out, was in the Up-and Out! Martel put his finger to his mouth and bit off the nail. He looked at the now-queer finger, and sighed to himself.

He stepped toward the city gate, slipping his hand into his jacket and running up his muscular strength to four times normal. He started to scan, and then realized that his instruments were masked. Might as well take all the chances at once, he thought.

The watcher stopped him with a searching Wire. The sphere thumped suddenly against Mattel's chest.

"Are you a Man?" said the unseen voice. (Martel would have known that as a Scanner in haberman condition, his own field-charge would have illuminated the sphere.)

"I am a Man." Martel knew that the timbre of his voice had been good; he hoped that it would not be taken for that of a Manshonjagger or a Beast or an Unforgiven one, who with mimicry sought to enter the cities and ports of Mankind.

"Name, number, rank, purpose, function, time departed."

"Martel." He had to remember his old number, not Scanner 34. "Sunward 4234, 182nd Year of Space. Rank, rising Subchief." That was no lie, but his substantive rank. "Purpose, personal and lawful within the limits of this city. No function of the Instrumentality. Departed Chief Outport 2019 hours." Everything now depended on whether he was believed, or would be checked against Chief Outport.

The voice was flat and routine: "Time desired within the city."

Martel used the standard phrase: "Your Honorable sufferance is requested."

He stood in the cool night air, waiting. Far above him, through a gap in the mist, he could see the poisonous glittering in the sky of Scanners. The stars are my enemies, he thought: I have mastered the stars but they hate me. Ho, that sounds Ancient! Like a Book. Too much cranching.

The voice returned: "Sunward 4234 dash 182 rising Subchief Martel, enter the lawful gates of the city. Welcome. Do you desire food, raiment, money, or companionship?" The voice had no hospitality in it, just business. This was certainly different from entering a city in a Scanner's role!

Then the petty officers came out, and threw their beltlights in their fretful faces, and mouthed their words with preposterous deference, shouting against the stone deafness of a Scanner's ears. So that was the way that a Subchief was treated: matter of fact, but not bad. Not bad.

Martel replied: "I have that which I need, but beg of the city a favor. My friend Adam Stone is here. I desired to see him, on urgent and personal lawful affairs."

The voice replied: "Did you have an appointment with Adam Stone?"

"No."

"The city will find him. What is his number?"

"I have forgotten it."

"You have forgotten it? Is not Adam Stone a Magnate of the Instrumentality? Are you truly his friend?"

"Truly." Martel let a little annoyance creep into his voice. "Watcher, doubt me and call your Subchief."

"No doubt implied. Why do you not know the number? This must go into the record," added the voice.

"We were friends in childhood. He has crossed the—" Martel started to say "the Up-and-Out" and remembered that the phrase was current only among Scanners. "He has leapt from Earth to Earth, and has just now returned. I knew him well and I seek him out. I have word of his kith. May the Instrumentality protect us!"

"Heard and believed. Adam Stone will be searched."

At a risk, though a slight one, of having the sphere sound an alarm for non-human, Martel cut in on his Scanner speaker within his jacket. He saw the trembling needle of light await his words and he started to write on it with his blunt finger. That won't work, he thought, and had a moment's panic until he found his comb, which had a sharp enough tooth to write. He wrote: "Emergency none. Martel Scanner calling

Parizianski Scanner."

The needle quivered and the reply glowed and faded out: "Parizianski Scanner on duty and D. C. Calls taken by Scanner Relay."

Martel cut off his speaker.

Parizianski was somewhere around. Could he have crossed the direct way, right over the city wall, setting off the alert, and invoking official business when the petty officers overtook him in mid-air? Scarcely. That meant that a number of other Scanners must have come in with Parizianski, all of them pretending to be in search of a few of the tenuous pleasures which could be enjoyed by a haberman, such as the sight of the newspictures or the viewing of beautiful women in the Pleasure Gallery. Parizianski was around, but he could not have moved privately, because Scanner Central registered him on duty and recorded his movements city by city.

The voice returned. Puzzlement was expressed in it. "Adam Stone is found and awakened. He has asked pardon of the Honorable, and says he knows no Martel. Will you see Adam Stone in the morning? The city will bid you welcome."

Martel ran out of resources. It was hard enough mimicking a man without having to tell lies in the guise of one. Martel could only repeat: "Tell him I am Martel. The husband of Luci."

"It will be done."

Again the silence, and the hostile stars, and the sense that Parizianski was somewhere near and getting nearer; Martel felt his heart beating faster. He stole a glimpse at his chestbox and set his heart down a point. He felt calmer, even though he had not been able to scan with care.

The voice this time was cheerful, as though an annoyance had been settled: "Adam Stone consents to see you. Enter Chief Downport, and welcome."

The little sphere dropped noiselessly to the ground and the wire whispered away into the darkness. A bright arc of narrow light rose from the ground in front of Martel and swept through the city to one of the higher towers—apparently a hostel, which Martel had never entered. Martel plucked his aircoat to his chest for ballast, stepped heel-and-toe on the beam, and felt himself whistle through the air to an entrance window which sprang up before him as suddenly as a devouring mouth.

A tower guard stood in the doorway. "You are awaited, sir. Do you bear weapons; sir?"

"None," said Martel, grateful that he was relying on his own strength.

The guard let him past the check-screen. Martel noticed the quick flight of a warning across the screen as his instruments registered and identified him as a Scanner. But the guard had not noticed it.

The guard stopped at a door. "Adam Stone is armed. He is lawfully armed by authority of the Instrumentality and by the liberty of this city. All those who enter are given warning."

Martel nodded in understanding at the man and went in.

Adam Stone was a short man, stout and benign. His grey hair rose stiffly from a low forehead. His whole face was red and merry looking. He looked like a jolly guide from the Pleasure Gallery, not like a man who had been at the edge of the Up-and-Out, righting the Great Pain without haberman protection.

He stared at Martel. His look was puzzled, perhaps a little annoyed, but not hostile.

Martel came to the point. "You do not know me. I lied. My name is Martel, and I mean you no harm. But I lied. I beg the Honorable gift of your hospitality. Remain armed. Direct your weapon against me—"

Stone smiled: "I am doing so," and Martel noticed the small

Wirepoint in Stone's capable plump hand.

"Good. Keep on guard against me. It will give you confidence in what I shall say. But do, I beg you, give us a screen of privacy. I want no casual lookers. This is a matter of life and death."

"First: whose life and death?" Stone's face remained calm, his voice even.

"Yours, and mine, and the worlds'."

"You are cryptic but I agree." Stone called through the doorway: "Privacy please." There was a sudden hum, and all the little noises of the night quickly vanished from the air of the room.

Said Adam Stone: "Sir, who are you? What brings you here?"

"I am Scanner Thirty-four."

"You a Scanner. I don't believe it."

For answer, Martel pulled his jacket open, showing his chestbox. Stone looked up at him, amazed. Martel explained:

"I am cranched. Have you never seen it before?"

"Not with men. On animals. Amazing! But—what do you want?"

"The truth. Do you fear me?"

"Not with this," said Stone, grasping the Wirepoint. "But I shall tell you the truth."

"Is it true that you have conquered the Great Pain?"

Stone hesitated, seeking words for an answer.

"Quick, can you tell me how you have done it, so that I may believe you?"

"I have loaded the ships with life."

"Life?"

"Life. I don't know what the great pain is, but I did find

that in the experiments, when I sent out masses of animals or plants, the life in the center of the mass lived longest. I built ships—small ones, of course—and sent them out with rabbits, with monkeys—"

"Those are Beasts?"

"Yes. With small Beasts. And the Beasts came back unhurt. They came back because the walls of the ships were filled with life. I tried many kinds, and finally found a sort of life which lives in the waters. Oysters. Oyster-beds. The outermost oyster died in the Great Pain. The inner ones lived. The passengers were unhurt."

"But they were Beasts?"

"Not only Beasts. Myself."

"You!"

"I came through Space alone. Through what you call the Up-and-Out, alone. Awake and sleeping. I am unhurt. If you do not believe me, ask your brother Scanners. Come and see my ship in the morning. I will be glad to see you then, along with your brother Scanners. I am going to demonstrate before the Chiefs of the Instrumentality."

Martel repeated his question: "You came here alone?"

Adam Stone grew testy: "Yes, alone. Go back and check your Scanner's register if you do not believe me. You never put me in a bottle to cross space."

Martel's face was radiant. "I believe you now. It is true. No more Scanners. No more habermans. No more cranching."

Stone looked significantly toward the door.

Martel did not take the hint. "I must tell you that—"

"Sir, tell me in the morning. Go enjoy your cranch. Isn't it supposed to be pleasure? Medically I know it well. But not in practice."

"It is pleasure. It's normality—for a while. But listen. The

Scanners have sworn to destroy you, and your work."

"What!"

"They have met and have voted and sworn. You will make Scanners unnecessary, they say. You will bring the Ancient Wars back to the world, if Scanning is lost and the Scanners live in vain!"

Adam Stone was nervous but kept his wits about him: "You're a Scanner. Are you going to kill me—or try?"

"No, you fool. I have betrayed the Confraternity. Call guards the moment I escape. Keep guards around you. I will try to intercept the killer."

Martel saw a blur in the window. Before Stone could turn, the Wirepoint was whipped out of his hand. The blur solidified and took form as Parizianski.

Martel recognized what Parizianski was doing: High speed.

Without thinking of his cranch, he thrust his hand to his chest, set himself up to High speed too. Waves of fire, like the Great Pain, but hotter, flooded over him. He fought to keep his face readable as he stepped in front of Parizianski and gave the sign,

Top Emergency.

Parizianski spoke, while the normally-moving body of Stone stepped away from them as slowly as a drifting cloud: "Get out of my way. I am on a mission."

"I know it. I stop you here and now. Stop. Stop. Stop. Stone is right."

Parizianski's lips were barely readable in the haze of pain which flooded Martel. (He thought: God, God. God of the Ancients! Let me hold on! Let me live under Overload just long enough!) Parizianski was saying: "Get out of my way. By order of the Confraternity, get out of my way!" And Parizianski gave the sign, Help I demand in the name of my duty!

Martel choked for breath in the syrup-like air. He tried one last time: "Parizianski, friend, friend, my friend. Stop. Stop." (No Scanner had ever murdered Scanner before.)

Parizianski made the sign: You are unfit for duty, and I will take over.

Martel thought, "For first time in the world!" as he reached over and twisted Parizianski's Brainbox up to Overload. Parizianski's eyes glittered in terror and understanding. His body began to drift down toward the floor.

Martel had just strength enough to reach his own Chestbox. As he faded into haberman or death, he knew not which, he felt his fingers turning on the control of speed, turning down. He tried to speak, to say, "Get a Scanner, I need help, get a Scanner...."

But the darkness rose about him, and the numb silence clasped him.

Martel awakened to see the face of Luci near his own.

He opened his eyes wider, and found that he was hearing—hearing the sound of her happy weeping, the sound of her chest as she caught the air back into her throat.

He spoke weakly: "Still cranched? Alive?"

Another face swam into the blur beside Luci's. It was Adam Stone. His deep voice rang across immensities of space before coming to Mattel's hearing. Mattel tried to read Stone's lips, but could not make them out. He went back to listening to the voice:

"...not cranched. Do you understand me? Not cranched!"

Mattel tried to say: "But I can hear! I can feel!" The others got his sense if not his words.

Adam Stone spoke again:

"You have gone back through the Haberman. I put you back first. I didn't know how it would work in practice, but I had the theory all worked out. You don't think the Instrumentality would waste the Scanners, do you? You go back to normality. We are letting the habermans die as fast as the ships come in. They don't need to live any more. But we are restoring the Scanners. You are the first. Do you understand? You are the first. Take it easy, now."

Adam Stone smiled. Dimly behind Stone, Mattel thought that he saw the face of one of the Chiefs of the Instrumentality. That face, too, smiled at him, and then both faces disappeared upward and away.

Martel tried to lift his head, to scan himself. He could not. Luci stared at him, calming herself, but with an expression of loving perplexity. She said,

"My darling husband! You're back again, to stay!"

Still, Martel tried to see his box. Finally he swept his hand across his chest with a clumsy motion. There was nothing there. The instruments were gone. He was back to normality but still alive.

In the deep weak peacefulness of his mind, another troubling thought took shape. He tried to write with his finger, the way that Luci wanted him to, but he had neither pointed fingernail nor Scanner's Tablet. He had to use his voice. He summoned up his strength and whispered:

"Scanners?"

"Yes, darling? What is it?"

"Scanners?"

"Scanners. Oh, yes, darling, they're all right. They had to arrest some of them for going into High Speed and running away. But the Instrumentality caught them all—all those on the ground—and they're happy now. Do you know, darling," she laughed, "some of them didn't want to be restored to normality. But Stone and his Chiefs persuaded them."

"Vomact?"

"He's fine, too. He's staying cranched until he can be

          SCANNERS LIVE IN VAIN

restored. Do you know, he has arranged for Scanners to take new jobs. You're all to be Deputy Chiefs for Space. Isn't that nice? But he got himself made Chief for Space. You're all going to be pilots, so that your fraternity and guild can go on. And Chang's getting changed right now. You'll see him soon."

Her face turned sad. She looked at him earnestly and said: "I might as well tell you now. You'll worry otherwise. There has been one accident. Only one. When you and your friend called on Adam Stone, your friend was so happy that he forgot to scan, and he let himself die of Overload."

"Called on Stone?"

"Yes. Don't you remember? Your friend."

He still looked surprised, so she said:

"Parizianski."

END